Christmas Started That Way

An original Christmas poem collection

Jerry Botta

Christmas Started That Way

Lo, in a manger... away from all danger,
    Asleep, on a bed of hay;
Through this baby unknown... God's love would be shown,
    Christmas started that way.

Shepherds drew near to worship with praise,
    Wise men came from afar;
Searching for answers, promises... hope,
    They decided to follow His star.

That journey would lead to a manger... a Lamb,
    The Cross was the price He would pay;
Forgiveness of sin... new life to begin,
    Christmas started that way.

So, which star have you chosen to follow,
    As you journey through life everyday?
Come to the manger... away from all danger,

Yes, Christmas started that way!

Jerry Botta ~ Christmas 1997.

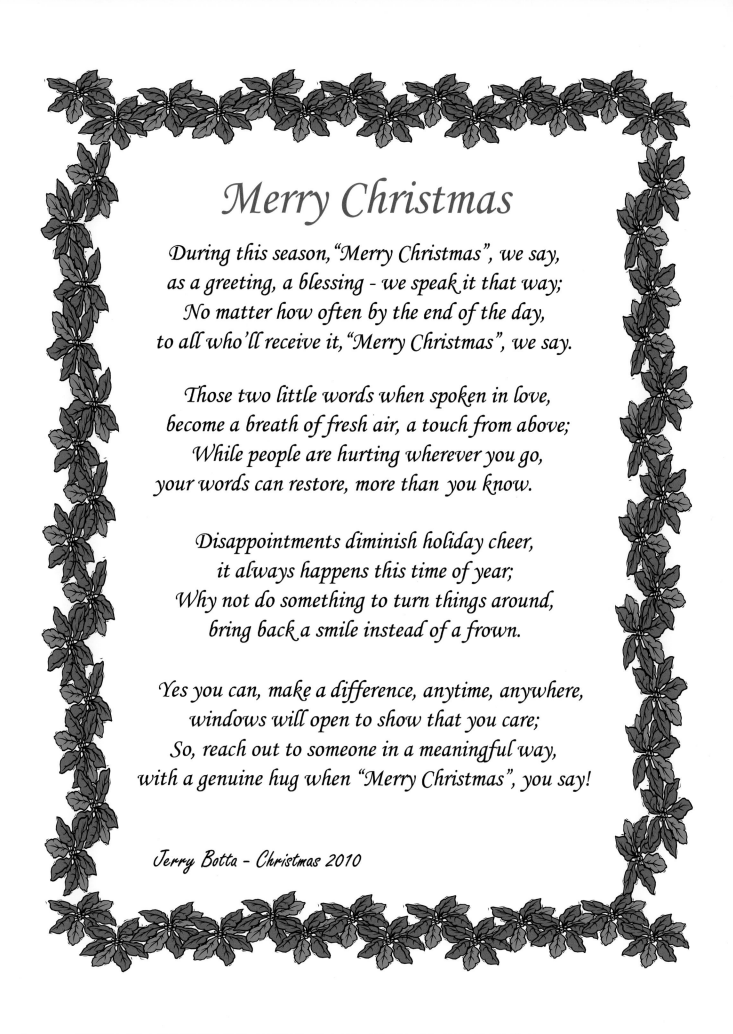

Merry Christmas

During this season, "Merry Christmas", we say,
as a greeting, a blessing - we speak it that way;
No matter how often by the end of the day,
to all who'll receive it, "Merry Christmas", we say.

Those two little words when spoken in love,
become a breath of fresh air, a touch from above;
While people are hurting wherever you go,
your words can restore, more than you know.

Disappointments diminish holiday cheer,
it always happens this time of year;
Why not do something to turn things around,
bring back a smile instead of a frown.

Yes you can, make a difference, anytime, anywhere,
windows will open to show that you care;
So, reach out to someone in a meaningful way,
with a genuine hug when "Merry Christmas", you say!

Jerry Botta - Christmas 2010

Christmastime

Christmastime means many things,
  loving, giving, having fun;
A time with friends and family,
  a season has begun.

Cold and snowy days ahead,
  winter here at last;
Turkeys roasting, parties hosting,
  reminders of the past.

Children growing, fires glowing,
  another year blows by;
Church bells ringing, choirs singing,
  a tear comes to your eye.

Yes, Christmastime means many things,
  loving, giving, having fun;
But most of all we celebrate,
  the Gift, of God's own Son!

Christmas 2012
  Jerry Botta

God's blessing makes life rich

Proverbs 10:22

The Best Gift of All

Bethlehem-town was busy that night,
    unaware of a star shining clearly and bright;
Mary grew tired, weary and worn,
    then in a stable, Jesus was born.

No doctors or nurses, no medical care,
    just a few shepherds, soon would be there;
Kneeling, they worshipped this baby, so small,
    it turned out to be, the best gift of all.

They followed a sign, away from the crowd,
    you see, God honors the humble while resisting the proud;
Awed in His presence without knowing His name,
    from that moment on, they were never the same.

Yes, signs are still given throughout life, everyday,
    to help you to find a new, better way;
This Christmas, respond, to God's love, to His call,
    it will turn out to be -- the best gift of all!

Christmas 2008
Jerry Botta

Only a Drum ~ Only a Joy

What gift can I give Lord, this Christmas, to You?
　　Something of value, innocent, true;
Only a drum, only a toy,
　　But, it's all that I have ~ I'm just a boy.

Wise men and kings brought treasures of old,
　　Perfumes and herbs, the finest of gold;
My gift is so small, a drum and a toy,
　　But, it's all that I have ~ I'm just a boy.

I'll play to announce Your message so clear,
　　Stop, look and listen ~ Christmas is here;
That's why You came, long ago, to this earth,
　　To bring us new life through the gift of Your birth.

So, thanks, for receiving my gift from the start,
　　Because what I give ~ I give from my heart;
When motives are right ~ to You, that brings joy,

If only a drum and only a toy.

Jerry Botta　Christmas, 2006

Trust God from the bottom of your heart;
  don't try to figure out everything on your own.

Listen for God's voice in everything you do,
  everywhere you go;
he's the one who will keep you on track.

Proverbs 3:5,6

Hopes and Fears

We all have them you know, our hopes and our fears,
    more so around Christmas, with the passing of years;
Hopes for the future, perhaps a dream will come true,
    fears for tomorrow, what to say, what to do.

You see, hopes unfulfilled engender more fears,
    disappointments result in frustration and tears;
Listen, only the Lord can reveal what is best,
    He said, "come to Me with your burdens and I'll give you rest".

So what are the hopes that set you apart,
    along with the fears you hold in your heart?
Yes, there's a Savior Who has you in sight,
    He alone is the answer to making things right.

Remember, "yet in the dark street shineth,
    The Everlasting Light;
the hopes and fears of all the years,
    are met in Thee, tonight".

Merry Christmas 2011
Jerry Botta

"Let your light so shine before men
that they may see you good deeds
and praise your father in heaven".

Matthew 5:6

The Candle of Christmas

Through the dark hours... in the still of the night,
      From a distance is seen... a candle so bright;
Not an object of beauty... like an angel with wings,
      Only a candle... and the light that it brings.

In times of confusion... crises and fear,
      Hope is restored... when a candle is near;
Yet, on a shelf... for years it may sit,
      A candle is useless... unless it is lit.

Your life, like a candle... touching many each day,
      Gives warmth and direction... as you walk in His way;
This Christmas, shine forth... in darkness, give sight,
      You are the candle... He is the light.

Yes, God uses candles... helping all men to see,
      His love and His blessing... what He made life to be;
His plan is eternal, His purpose... unfurled,
      The Candle of Christmas... is

The Light of the World.

Jerry Botta
Christmas, 1991

The best time of the year

Christmas is the Best Time of the Year

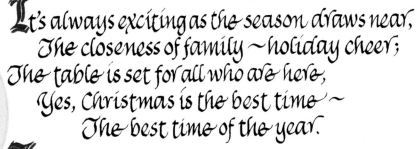

It's always exciting as the season draws near,
  The closeness of family ~ holiday cheer;
The table is set for all who are here,
  Yes, Christmas is the best time ~
    The best time of the year.

There are presents to wrap and cookies to bake,
  Candles to light, fires to make ;
Carols to sing and music to play,
  Celebration and joy on this one special day.

It all started, you know, when Jesus was born,
  God sent His Son that first Christmas morn;
Into a world steeped in sadness and sin,
  His gift was forgiveness ~ peace from within.

From baby to child, a boy to a man,
  Each step in His life fulfilling God's plan;
Now, even to you, His love will appear,
  Simply, believe ~ your past will be clear.

Yes, it's exciting as the season draws near,
  Knowing the reason brings holiday cheer;
So, cherish the moments with those you hold dear,
  For, Christmas is the best time ~
    The best time of the year!

Jerry Botta ~ Christmas, 2005

Christmas is Here

Angels rejoiced on the night of His birth,
   That moment in time when God came to earth;
Scorned by a world in confusion and shame,
   Unwanted, rejected... few knew His name.

In Nazareth, He was called the "carpenter's son",
   The Cross was ahead... much work to be done;
Deaf ears would open, blind men would see,
   God's plan was in motion... all could be free.

Have you received Him as Savior today,
   This One Who first came... to take sin away?
He knows every trial, He'll calm every fear,
   Simply, open your heart...

Christmas is here!

Jerry Botta ~ Christmas, 1995.

he who refreshes others
will himself be refreshed.

Proverbs 11:25

A Gift Fit for a King

One Gift was given... that first Christmas morn,
    In humble surroundings... the Savior was born;
Later they came... three wise men of old,
    Presenting their treasures... myrrh, frankincense, gold.

The bitter, the fragrant... the costly of life,
    Prophetical signs of anguish and strife;
Bowing, they worshipped and gave all they had,
    There in God's presence... rejoicing, not sad.

What gift do you hold in your hands this day?
    Stop clutching... release it... give it away;
Your life can touch many as a channel of love,
    Reflecting His goodness... shaped from above.

Yes, the Creator... will make all things new,
    Because there is nothing... God cannot do;
Come to Him now... open hands only bring,
    He'll make _you_ a gift...

a gift.... fit.... for a King!

Jerry Botta
Christmas, 1994

Come as a Child

What do you want for Christmas this year,
     One special gift ... some holiday cheer ?
A chance to help others as never before,
     The warmth of a family ... love, to outpour ?

Times have been difficult, wearisome ... rough,
     Growing concerns ... there won't be enough ;
Dreams, all but shattered, expectancy ... lost,
     Instead of rejoicing ... counting the cost.

Yet, through the mist ... see a glimmer of light,
     The message of Christmas shines ever so bright ;
Prophets foretold God's love would be shown,
     Lo, in a manger ... His Gift was made known.

He came to give life and peace from within,
     Love, hope and joy ... freedom from sin ;
His promise to guide is yours for today,
     Ask and receive ... don't turn Him away.

So, what do you want for Christmas this year,
     One special gift ... some holiday cheer ?
Perhaps, to know Him ... Who is gentle and mild,
     Then, open your heart ... and come as a child.

Jerry Botta ~ Christmas, 1993

And there were shepherds living out in the fields nearby, keeping watch over their flocks at night. An angel of the Lord appeared to them, and the glory of the Lord shone around them, and they were terrified. But the angel said to them, "Do not be afraid. I bring you good news of great joy that will be for all people.

Today in the town of David a Savior has been born to you; he is Christ the Lord. This will be a sign to you: You will find a baby wrapped in cloths and lying in a manger."

Luke 2:8-12

G·L·O·R·Y

— to the Newborn King

Breath of heaven come to earth,
      The world rejoices at Your birth;
God is here . . . O shout and sing,
      Glory to the newborn King.

In a manger He began,
      To fulfill the Father's plan;
Forgiveness, love and life to bring,
      Glory to the newborn King.

Do you need a brand new start?
      He alone can mend your heart;
Hope and joy within will ring,
      Yes, glory to the newborn King!

Jerry Botta, Christmas 1996.

Bethlehem's Star

Wise men and shepherds worshipped that night,
    A Babe in a manger... born to bring light;
Rejected by many... no room at the inn,
    The Savior had come... to take away sin.

High in the sky... on an evening so clear,
    God's signal was given... look up and draw near;
Yet, few were aware of His miracle birth,
    Few understood His coming to earth.

Perhaps you are burdened with care and concern,
    His presence and glory... you cannot discern;
Reaching out in His love He longs to impart,
    Hope and forgiveness... which flow from His heart.

Yes, God is at work in your everyday life,
    The peace that He gives will calm every strife;
He'll show you a sign... wherever you are;
    Lift your eyes with rejoicing to...

Bethlehem's Star.

Jerry Botta
Christmas 1992

*"So the Master is going to give you
a sign anyway. Watch for this: A girl
who is presently a virgin will get pregnant.
She'll bear a son and name him Immanuel
(God-With-Us)"*.

Isaiah 7:14

Immanuel

All is well, all is well,
The Lord has come and all is well;
Go and tell, all is well,
God with us... Immanuel.

Sound the trumpet, ring the bell,
Shout the news, all is well;
To every village, farm and dell,
The Lord has come and all is well.

So, is it well...with your soul?
He alone can make you whole;
Receive His love, forgiveness too,
He came for all, including you.

Indeed, for you... He came as well,
New life and peace within to dwell;
He will restore your broken shell,
And you will know...that all is well.

Yes, all is well, all is well,
The Lord has come and all is well;
Sound the trumpet, ring the bell,
Rejoice in Him... Immanuel.

Jerry Botta ~ Christmas 1999.

Unto You Is Born A Savior... This Day

Speechless, astonished, trembling ... they feared,
When suddenly to shepherds, an angel appeared;
"Don't be afraid ... for, not far away,
Unto you is born, a Savior ... this day".

Excited, inspired ... at the sound of that voice,
They made a decision ... after all, it's a choice;
Searching, they found the place where He lay,
Yes, "Unto you is born, a Savior ... this day".

There in a manger ... God Himself had drawn near,
In the form of a baby ... a picture, so clear;
Not more religion but a new, living way,
"Unto you is born, a Savior ... this day".

So, are you willing like those shepherds of old,
To search 'til you find what the angel foretold?
Don't be afraid ... He's not far away,
For, "Unto you is born a Savior...
    this day!"

Jerry Botta ~ Christmas, 1998

Sleep, O Sleep... Most Holy Child

Sleep, o sleep, most holy Child.
   In Your mother's arms so caring;
Rest, o rest, sweet little Child,
   What lies ahead, God is preparing.

         You must grow, become a man,
            Yes, fulfill the Father's plan;
         Pure, transparent, unbeguiled,
            Sleep, o sleep, most holy Child.

For this cause, to earth You came;
   Without blemish, undefiled;
Born to live, die to give,
   Sleep, o sleep, most holy Child.

         So now to You my hands I raise;
            One so precious, meek and mild;
         Receive my worship, love and praise,
            As You sleep, o sleep, most holy Child!

Jerry Botta ~ Christmas 2003.

Rejoice in the True Prince of Peace

Baffled, bewildered, in tears ... he would be,
   When Mary told Joseph, "I'm pregnant, you see;"
"But why, tell me why ... how can this be,
   What of the promise between you and me?"

That night in a dream an angel did say,
   "Don't worry, fear not ... it will all be ok;
In time there will be a miracle birth,
   Jesus, Messiah ... God coming to earth."

Bethlehem's journey grew weary and long,
   Hopes would be crushed should something go wrong;
Then a knock on the door drew a voice from within,
   "Sorry, sold out ... no room at the inn."

Outside in a stable...the Savior was born,
  Away, in a manger...that first Christmas morn;
A new era in history had then just begun,
  God had given His very own Son.

That Son would be given again...at the cross,
  A ransom for sin...redemption for loss;
He came to mend lives, to set people free,
  Free to become all He wants us to be.

So, is this season the time you'll open your heart,
  To Him who alone can give a new start?
His love is unending...it never will cease,
  This Christmas rejoice...in the true Prince of Peace!

The True Prince of Peace

Jerry Botta ~ Christmas, 2001.

For God so loved the world that he gave
his only Son, so that everyone who believes
in him will not perish, but have eternal life.

John 3:16

It's Never Too Late

December '04 ~ another year has gone by,
   Incidentally, it's true ~ time really does fly;
Christmas already? Are you sure? Can it wait?
   No, enter the season ~ it's never too late.

So many problems, so much to do,
   Miracles needed, not just a few;
Resources dwindling ~ like, closing a gate,
   Yet, somehow you make it ~ it's never too late.

Listen, God wants to bless, your future ~ your fate,
   Give peace through the pressures and fears that you hate;
Life can be different ~ wonderful ~ great,
   Simply, come to the Savior ~ it's never too late!

Christmas/04, Jerry Botta

A Servant, A Savior, A Son

A Servant, a Savior, a Son,
God's gift to the world, wrapped in one;
From a manger He grew to touch everyone's need,
in serving, He taught the true way to lead.

No other could say, "I am The Way",
the cross was the price a Savior would pay;
This was the reason for His coming to earth,
that very first Christmas, a miracle birth.

An obedient son, from beginning to end,
more than a carpenter, teacher and friend;
He said, "all who are weary, come to Me and find rest",
you see; putting Him first allows your life to be blessed.

So, as you journey along, some decisions are tough,
just getting through Christmas can be trouble enough;
But if, indeed, you do want Him to be number One,
then, say yes to a Servant, a Savior, a Son!

Christmas, 2007
Jerry Botta

A Season of Sharing, Holiday Cheer

We celebrate Christmas toward the end of the year,
    a season of sharing, holiday cheer;
A time to remember God's blessings, His love,
    a moment to worship His Gift from above.

Yet, with each season comes the bitter, the sweet,
    in joyous occasions realities meet;
As dinner is served you become more aware,
    around the Christmas table, you see an empty chair.

Someone is missing, a loved one, a friend,
    no greetings, embraces, no presents to send;
Last Christmas was different, that someone was here,
    a season of sharing, holiday cheer.

You're reminded how quickly the years seem to fly,
    like, good morning, hello - good evening, goodbye;
Yes, life is a journey, God's gift to be sure,
    with signposts and signals - to make you secure.

So, remember God's blessings, be touched by His love,
    take a moment to worship His Gift from above;
Let the meaning of Christmas be special, be clear,
    in this season of sharing, holiday cheer.

Christmas 2009 - Jerry Botta

In loving memory of Teresa Amati; Albert Botta; Claudio Fluterio;
Lola Genovese; Joseph LoMonica; Tom Mandic; Kim Meglio;
Alanna Moorman; Esther Pearce; Rina Piou; Dennis Soccorso;
Angelo and Josephine Terameo; Roberto Terminella

A Time of Rejoicing and Cheer

Never before has Christmas meant more...
Than what it means this year;
A time of new life, a time of new love;
A time of rejoicing and cheer.

When Jesus was born that first Christmas morn,
God's life and love had drawn near;
Through this baby, so small... forgiveness for all,
A time of rejoicing and cheer.

That's why He came, to give His life and His love,
For all who are willing to hear;
"Come unto Me, I'll not turn you away",
Yes, a time of rejoicing and cheer.

So, what meaning has Christmas for you, this year?
Is your path still uncertain, unclear?
Simply, open your heart to His life and His love;
To a time of rejoicing and cheer!

Jerry Botta ~ Christmas, 2000

Guide us to Thy Perfect Light

"Peace on earth, good will toward men",
   yes, Christmas is here, here once again;
Celebration, love, hope and good cheer,
   a time to enjoy those you hold dear.

But Christmas somehow seems different this year,
   marred by deception, confusion and fear;
Wrongful decisions, painful divisions,
   the future . . uncertain, unclear.

Many roads invite you to travel,
   on your journey through life everyday;
Many problems then to unravel,
   only God can show you the way.

So, which path will you choose to follow,
   like the shepherds that first Christmas night?
Listen to the carol of "We Three Kings,
   guide us . . to Thy Perfect Light"!

Christmas 2013
Jerry Botta

A New Christmas Love

My Christmas tree stands beautiful and tall,
　　　Everyone loves it, especially children, one and all.
It's filled with happiness, peace, joy and love;
　　　Christmas gifts that only come from above.

Kids playing on our sidewalk stop to look in,
　　　They hear music and laughter,
　　　　　They see ornaments made of silver and tin.

As you walk into the room to see this tree tall and stout,
　　　You soon realize what Christmas is really about.

It's about loving and giving ~ of gifts not made of gold ~
　　　Childhood pictures, memories of old.

"Not for me", you may say, "no joy of the past,
　　　Only sorrows and tears ~ hurts that would last."

"Many years I have wasted ~ with nothing to show,
　　　And now I am told I must reap what I sow."

But look deeper, for God's Spirit will cause you to see,
　　　That He can change anyone ~ even you ~ even me.

His love was shown on a cross ~ on a tree;
　　　So that we could become all He wants us to be.

Look to Him now and be free from the past;
　　　His Spirit will do it and yes, it will last.

Come to the Saviour who was sent from above;
　　　Come and receive
　　　　　　A New Christmas Love.

Jerry Botta
Christmas, 1990

Did You Know?

Mary, did you know, your baby boy would one day walk on water,
  Mary, did you know, your baby boy would heal a son and daughter?
Did you know when you held Him close, the truth, about His birth,
  Did you know, when you kissed His face that God had come to earth?
Mary, did you know?

Shepherds, did you know, you would be the ones to watch your flocks by night,
  Shepherds, did you know, you would be the ones to see that guiding light?
Did you know, you were the chosen ones to worship and bow down,
  Did you know, He was "The Chosen One" ~ a King without a crown?
Shepherds, did you know?

Wise men, did you know, you would be the ones to travel from afar,
  Wise men, did you know, you would be the ones to see His shining star?
Did you know your hands would hold ~ perfume, myrrh and gold,
  Did you know His hands would hold ~ a future yet untold?
Wise men, did you know?

Child, did you know, that Jesus came for you,
  Child, did you know, that He can see you through?
Did you know He'll keep His word ~ He will return one day,
  Then, did you know the Savior ~ The Truth, The Life ~ The Way?

Child, did you know?

Jerry Botta ~ Christmas, 2002

The Message of Christmas

What do you remember of Christmas as a child,
    the excitement, the fun, all the kids running wild?
Perhaps when an era was more enjoyable too,
    without cell phones or Facebook, now what would we do?

The message of Christmas remains always the same,
    God's love was made known through Jesus, by name;
Then, times were fearful, much like today,
    the choices: rejection or new life to stay.

Yes, everything changed from the world you once knew,
    yet, that glimmer of light keeps shining through;
So, this season respond, afresh and anew,
    to the message of Christmas, that... God loves, you!

Christmas 2014
Jerry Botta